ITALIAN: THE COMPLETE TRAVEL PHRASEBOOK

The Complete Italian Phrasebook for Traveling to Italy.

+ 1000 Phrases for Accommodations, Shopping, Eating, Traveling, and much more!

By Erica Stewart

ERICA STEWART

© **Copyright 2015**

All rights reserved. No part of this book may be reproduced or transmitted in any form or by any means, electronically or mechanically, including photocopy, recording, or by and information storage or retrieval system, without the written permission from the publisher, except in the case of brief quotations embodied in critical articles or reviews.

Trademarks are the property of their respective holders. When used, trademarks are for the benefit of the trademark owner only.

DISCLAIMER

The information provided herein is stated to be truthful and consistent, in that any liability, in terms of inattention or otherwise, by any usage or abusage of any policies, processes, or directions contained within is the solitary and utter responsibility of the recipient reader. Under no circumstances will any legal responsibility or blame be held against the publisher for any reparation, damages, or monetary loss due to the information herein, either directly or indirectly. Respective authors hold all rights not held by publisher.

Note from the Author:

Traveling is one of the most enriching experiences, on so many levels. Being able to interact with the locals makes that experience even more enriching, allowing you to connect with new and interesting people, or even live or study overseas. Traveling is in essence a journey to become more open minded about the world, discovering amazing new people in the process.

As an educator for more than 20 years, I'm a fan of teaching languages to others. This book does not pretend to teach you a commanding knowledge of Italian, but is an assembly of the most fundamental phrases you will need when traveling to Italy.

Over the course of this book, I will convey enough knowledge of Italian so that you will be able to read, listen, and interact with people in these countries in a way that will inspire confidence. From here, practice will take you to a new level of accomplishments and a lifetime of enjoyment!

ERICA STEWART

Imagine heading out to Rome, Venice, Naples or Florence fully equipped to interact with the locals! I invite you to read on and begin a fascinating learning experience.

Best,

Erica Stewart

Chapter Index

Introduction 10

    Countries and territories where Italian is official 10

    Countries and territories where Italian has a significant/cultural presence 10

    Travel Ideas When Visiting Italy 11

    Culture 12

Differences with English 14

    Alphabet 14

    Phonology 14

    Grammar 15

    Vocabulary 15

Pronunciation 16

    Italian alphabet 17

    Diacritical marks 17

    Sounds of letters 18

    Consonantic clusters 20

    Some examples on stress patterns 20

Some Grammar 22

Articles 22

Some examples 24

Greetings 26

General Conversation 29

Numbers 31

Numbers from 10 to 100 in tens 34

Large numbers 34

Directions & Places 35

Transportation 38

Travelling Vocabulary 38

Means of Transportation 40

Taxi 40

Bus and Train 42

At the bus or train station 42

When will you be coming back? – Quando intende tornare? 43

On the bus or train 44

The Tube/subway 45

Planes 46

Checking in 46

Security 48

  In the departure lounge 48
  On the plane 49
  Things you might see 50
Eating out 52
 Dining Etiquette 52
 Vocabulary 53
  Eating and drinking 53
 At pub/bar 54
  Ordering drinks 54
  Ordering snacks and food 56
  Internet access 57
  Smoking 57
 At a restaurant 57
  Booking a table 57
  Ordering the meal 58
  During the meal 60
  Problems 61
 Paying the bill 61
Hotel and Accommodation 63
 Making a reservation 63

- *Checking availability* 63
- *Asking about facilities* 64
- *Discussing terms* 65
- Making the Booking 66
- Checking in 66
- Things you might see 68
- Checking out 68

Shopping 70
- Opening times 70
- Selecting goods 71
- Making payment 72
- Returns and complaints 73
- Things you might see 73
- Using a credit card 74

**** PREVIEW OTHER BOOKS BY THIS AUTHOR****.75

"Rome Travel Guide for Women" by Erica Stewart ...75

[Excerpt from the first Chapter – for complete book, please purchase on Amazon.com] 75

[Excerpt from the first Chapter – for complete book, please purchase on Amazon.com] 94

Introduction

Italian is a language spoken by about 60 million people mainly in Italy, Switzerland, San Marino and the Vatican City. It belongs to the Romance, or Neo-Latin, family, a group of languages that evolved from Latin, an Indo-European language spoken in Ancient Italy, more specifically in the city of Rome.

Countries and territories where Italian is official

- Italy
- Switzerland
- San Marino
- Vatican City

Countries and territories where Italian has a significant/cultural presence

- Malta
- Istria County (Croatia)
- Slovenian Istria (Slovenia)
- Corsica

Travel Ideas When Visiting Italy

- **Rome** – the capital city is an open-air museum of Roman history and Renaissance art. The Vatican City, featuring St. Peter's Basilica and the Vatican Museums, is also located within the city.
- **Milan** – the heart of Italian fashion and economics, Milan is world-wide renowned for its restaurants and boutiques, as well as for the La Scala opera house.
- **Venice** – built on more than 100 islands in the Venetian lagoon, the city is a masterpiece of architecture and one of the most popular tourist destinations in the world.
- **Florence** – most of the city still retains its Medieval buildings and streets, as well as numerous churches and towers. It also features some of the greatest works of art of the Renaissance period.
- **Naples** – internationally famous as the home of pizza, the city also has the largest historic centre in Europe and is close to culturally significant sites , including the Roman ruins of Pompeii and Herculaneum.
- **Turin** – the city was the first capital of Italy after its unification in 1861. Many historic cafés

and museums are located within its 19th century centre.
- **Sicily** – numerous Ancient Greek and Roman sites are located on the island, which is also famous for its cuisine and its natural beaches.

Culture

The population speaks Italian, a Romance language derived from Vulgar Latin and the Florentine language. Regional languages, known as dialects, are sometimes so distinct from the standard as to result mutually unintelligible. Although still spoken, especially amongst the elderly population, they are regarded as minority languages and are gradually disappearing.

Owing to its long and multifaceted history, Italy features more UNESCO World Heritage Sites than any other country in the world and more than 100000 monuments, from archaeological sites to castles and cathedrals. As the birthplace of the Roman Empire, Italy is filled with ruins from the Roman period, as well as Greek and Etruscan sites; as heart of the Renaissance, it boasts an enormous number of paintings, statues, and historic buildings.

Italian cuisine is one of the most famous in the world. Since the country wasn't unified until the late 1800s, every city and region developed its own specialities, drawing from the peninsula's great diversity of flora and fauna, and the rich and fertile soil. Even the smallest towns have at least one annual food festival.

Italy is also regarded as one of the leading fashion centres of the world, most notably in the city of Milan, and as the birthplace of opera: the Roman Arena of Verona, in Northern Italy, hosts hundreds of spectacles, operas, and concerts every year. In addition, the country is home to many music festivals, ranging from folk dances to jazz and rock concerts.

Differences with English

Italian is a Romance language and part of the larger Indo-European family. It is related to Spanish, French, Portuguese, and, to a lesser extent, Romanian. Apart from small changes in the vocabulary, Swiss Italian is completely intelligible with the kind spoken in Italy.

As a result of the country's history as a divided nation, Standard Italian is a purely linguistic concept: each region has its own variety, with differences being more pronounced in the southern part of the peninsula. However, they mostly boil down to vocabulary and shifts in pronunciation, and a basic knowledge of the standard is more than enough to understand and be understood anywhere.

Alphabet
The Italian alphabet has 21 letters. The letters j, k, w, x, y are used only in loanwords, foreign terms, and some Italian place-names. Punctuation largely corresponds to that of English.

Phonology
Italian has 5 vowel sounds and 20 consonant sounds. There is no distinction between long and short vowels.

All consonants except H can be either geminated or doubled, proving particularly difficult to pronounce correctly for an English speaker. However, unlike English, Italian pronunciation is decidedly consistent with the orthography.

Grammar

The Italian verb system is arguably more complex than that of English, namely because of the greater number of tenses. Unlike English, adjectives and pronouns are subject to number and gender declension; partly because of this, Italian word order is more flexible than English. The placement of adjectives and adverbials also tends to be reversed in comparison to English.

Vocabulary

English has acquired an extensive vocabulary from French and Latin and English speakers will likely recognise many Italian words, especially in specialised discourse. However, this also means they are more likely to encounter false cognates.

Pronunciation

Pronunciation is arguably the most important aspect of learning a language. Of course, you don't have to be able to pronounce everything perfectly to be understood, and it will take time to get used to the strange sounds that you have to produce.

Italian pronunciation is not too difficult compared to other languages, but some sounds, namely "gli", "gn", and "r", don't exist in English and may prove challenging at first. Remember, though, that most people will understand you even if your pronunciation is not perfect. Some may even think your foreign accent is charming.

A few basic rules regarding Italian pronunciation:

1. Most of the words are stressed in the second to last syllable.
2. When a word is stressed in the last syllable, the vowel bears a tonic accent (e.g.: caff<u>è</u>, perch<u>é</u>).
3. All consonants, except H, can be doubled.
4. You normally pronounce every letter in a word, except for the H which is always silent.

5. Generally, this is also true for diphthongs (a vowel preceded or followed by an unstressed I or U) as well.

Italian alphabet

Aa	Bb	Cc	Dd	Ee	Ff	Gg	Hh	Ii	Jj	Kk	Ll
Á	Bi	Ci	Di	é	Effe	Gi	Acca	I	I		lunga Cappa Elle

Mm	Nn	Oo	Pp	Qq	Rr	Ss	Tt	Uu	Vv	Ww
Emme	Enne	ó	Pi	Cu	Erre	Esse	Ti	U	Vi	Doppia vi

Xx Yy Zz

Ics Ipsilon Zeta

Diacritical marks

The grave accent [`] denotes stress in the last syllable. If the vowel bearing the accent is an E, it should be pronounced very open, as in "test".

The acute accent ['] denotes stress in the last syllable and is found only on the E. In this case, the vowel should be pronounced closed, as in "moment".

Sounds of letters

A – like "a" in "cat".

B – as in English.

C – like "k" in "key" when followed by "a", "o", and "u", like "ch" in "check" when followed by "i" and "e".

D – as in English, but without aspiration.

E – like "e" in "test" or "moment" depending on the word.

F – as in English.

G – like "g" in "game" when followed by "a", "o", and "u", like "j" in "Jack" when followed by "i" and "e".

H – always silent.

I – like "ee" in "free".

J - only found in loanwords. Same as in English.

K - only found in loanwords. Same as in English.

L – as in English.

M – as in English.

N – as in English.

O – like "o" in "closed" or "dog" depending on the context.

P – as in English, but without aspiration.

Q – like "k" in "key". Only found followed by "u".

R – like a Scottish R. Some people in Northern Italy may either pronounce it like "r" in French "rouge" or German "rot", or just drop it altogether.

S – like "z" in "zebra" between vowels and before a voiced consonants (b, d, g, v), like "s" in "sound" elsewhere.

T – as in English, but without aspiration.

U – like "oo" in "broom".

V – as in English.

W – only found in loanwords, same as in English. A few words like "water" (toilet) and Walter (a proper name) have it like "v".

X – only found in loanwords. Same as in English.

Y – only found in loanwords. Same as in English.

Z – like "ts" in "tsunami" when in the last syllable and when followed by –ia, -io, and –ie, roughly like "z" in "zebra" when in the first syllable and between two vowels.

Consonantic clusters

CH – like "k" in "key".

CI – like "ch" in "check".

GH – like "g" in "game".

GI – like "j" in "Jack".

GLI – found followed by "a", "o", "u", and "e", it is pronounced like a long or doubled "y" or like "ll" in Spanish "caballo".

GN – similar to "ny" in "canyon" or Spanish "señor".

QU – like "kw" in "awkward".

SC – like "sc" in "scold" when followed by "a", "o", "u". Like "sh" in "short" when followed by "e" and "i".

SCH – like "sc" in "scold".

Some examples on stress patterns

The bold parts are the ones to be stressed:

- **Do**ve sei **sta**to? (Where have you been?)
- **So**no an**da**to al **ci**nema. (I went to the cinema.)

- Vor**r**e**i** un caf**fè**. (I would like a coffe.)

- Hai **u**na **gran**de opportun**ità**. (You have a great opportunity.)

- **Mio** cu**g**ino ha più **li**bri di **mio** pa**pà**. (My cousin has more books than my dad.)

- I **piat**ti **so**no **sta**ti la**va**ti. (The dishes have been washed.)
- **La**vati le **ma**ni! (Wash your hands!)

Some Grammar

While Italian grammar is more complex than English, it is by no means insuperable. Perfect grammar takes years to fully master and even native speakers make mistakes once in a while. This section will serve as a short introduction to a feature of Italian grammar that proves particularly difficult for English speakers, namely nouns, articles, and their declension according to gender and number.

Articles

Where English only has two indefinite articles and one definite, Italian has up to seven. These are:

Indefinites:
Uno – used for masculine singular nouns beginning with Z or S + consonant. It also corresponds to the numeral "one".
Un – used for all other masculine singular nouns.
Una – used for feminine singular nouns beginning with a consonant.
Un' – elision of **una**, used for feminine singular nouns beginning with a vowel.

Definite   **singular:**
Lo – used for masculine nouns beginning with Z or S + consonant.
Il – used for all other masculine nouns beginning with a consonant.
La – used with feminine nouns beginning with a consonant.
L' – elision of either **lo** or **la**, it is used for masculine or feminine nouns beginning with a vowel.

Definite   **plural:**
Gli – used for masculine nouns beginning with a vowel, Z, GN, S + consonant.
I – used for masculine nouns beginning with any other consonant.
Le – used for any feminine noun.

Note: indefinite articles have no plural. In the case of an unspecified number of nouns the form **dei/delle** (equivalent to English "some") may be used.

Nouns and Adjectives

Just like in English, nouns have a gender and a number. Unlike English, however, adjectives must be declined according to the number and gender of the noun they refer to.
To further complicate things, where English has a

neutral gender for objects and animals alike, Italian assigns a specific gender (either masculine or feminine) to each of them. As a general rule, nouns ending in **–O** (singular) and **–I** (plural) are masculine, while those ending in **–A** (singular) and **–E** (plural) are feminine. As with every feature of Italian grammar this rule is prone to exception, so, for example, "tigre" (tiger) and "volpe" (fox) are feminine but "sole" (sun) is masculine, "dito" (finger) is masculine but "dita" (fingers) is feminine. All these must be learned through memorization.

Some examples

La volpe ros**sa** mangia **la** carne. (The red fox eats the meat.)

Lo studente impara **le** eccezioni della lingua italiana. (The student learns the exceptions of the Italian language.)

Le ragazz**e** leggono **un** manifest**o**. (The girls read a poster.)
I ragazz**i** leggono **una** vecchi**a** rivist**a**. (The boys read an old magazine.)

L'uomo indossa **una** giacca elegant**e**. (The man is wearing an elegant suit.)
Le sorell**e** portano scarp**e** elegant**i**. (The sisters are

wearing elegant shoes.)

Il grand**e** gigante gentil**e** cammina con **la** piccol**a** bambin**a** da**i** capell**i** biond**i**. (The tall, kind giant walks with the little child with blonde hair.)

Ide**e** verd**i** multicolor**i** dormono furiosamente. (Colourless green ideas sleep furiously.)

Greetings

I don't know about you, but every time I go out of my country I meet new people and sometimes even make friends. Meeting new people or friends starts by greeting them, so let's learn Italian greetings and customs.

Initial greetings are reserved, yet polite. A handshake works well for both men and women, although it is not uncommon to kiss a woman twice on the cheek if she is close to a relative or friend of yours. It is good manners to talk to older people or prominent figures using a formal, more polite form.

Once a relationship has developed, greeting become more personal: men may greet each other with a hug and a handshake and women kiss each other twice on the cheek starting with the right. Men and women usually exchange two kisses on the cheek as well.

Let's extend our Italian vocabulary and learn how to greet on the different parts of the day:

- Buongiorno! (Good morning/Good day!)

- Buonasera! (Good Afternoon/ Good evening!) (After 4 p.m.)
- Buonanotte! (Good night!) (Before going to bed or when leaving after a night out.)
- Note: the three forms above can be shortened respectively as "giorno", "sera", "notte".
- Ciao, come stai? (Hi, how are you?) (Informal)
- Salve, come stai? (Hello, how are you?) (Formal)
- Bene, grazie. (I'm ok, thank you)
- Benissimo/ alla grande!. (I'm fine/ I'm doing great!) (Formal/ informal)
- Non male. (Not too bad)
- Mi chiamo John, e tu? (My name is John, and yours?) (Informal)
- Mi chiamo John, e lei? (My name is John, and yours?) (Formal)
- Piacere di conoscerti. (Nice to meet you.) (Informal)
- Piacere di conoscerla. (Nice to meet you.) (Formal)
- Note: the two forms above are usually shortened as "piacere".
- Il piacere è mio. (The pleasure is all mine.) (Elegant/old fashioned)
- Ciao. (Goodbye.) (Informal)

- Arrivederci. (Goodbye). (Formal)
- A dopo. (See you later.)
- A domani. (See you tomorrow.)
- A presto. (See you soon.)
- Alla prossima. (See you next time.)
- Per favore/ per piacere. (Please.)
- Grazie. (Thank you.)
- Grazie mille. (Thank you very much.)

General Conversation

Now we know how to greet the people we talk with, but it would be a weird conversation if we only said hello and goodbye.

Read through the word lists on the following pages, and practise saying them aloud.

Let's see some simple conversational phrases:

- Dove stai andando? (Where are you going?) (Informal, singular)
- Dove sta andando? (Where are you going?) (Formal, singular)
- Dove state andando? (Where are you going?) (Plural)
- Come ti chiami? (What's your name?) (Informal)
- Come si chiama? (What's your name?) (Formal)
- Hai un soprannome? (Do you have a nickname?)
- Puoi chiamarmi Bob. (You can call me Bob.) (Singular)
- Potete chiamarmi Bob. (You can call me Bob.) (Plural)

- Qual è il tuo cognome? (What's your last name?)
- Potresti sillabarlo? (Could you spell it?) (Informal)
- Potrebbe sillabarlo? (Could you spell it?) (Formal)
- Vorrei presentarle alcuni amici... (Let me introduce you to some friends...) (Formal)
- Note: in informal contexts it is more common to use the form "lui/lei è ..." (this is ...).
- Lei è la mia ragazza. (She/this is my girlfriend.)
- Lui è il mio ragazzo. (He/this is my boyfriend.)
- Note: the term "fidanzato/a" is roughly equivalent to English "fiancé/e" and is generally used when things are getting serious.
- Sai il suo nome? (Do you know his/her name?) (Informal)
- Sa il suo nome? (Do you know his/her name?) (Formal)
- Come si chiama? (What's his/her name?)
- Parli italiano? (Do you speak Italian?) (Informal)
- Parla italiano? (Do you speak Italian? (Formal)
- Parlate italiano? (Do you speak Italian? (Plural)
- Solo un po'. (Just a little bit.)
- Lo sto imparando. (I'm learning.)

- Lo capisco meglio di come lo parlo. (I understand more than I speak.)
- Ho appena iniziato a studiarlo... (I've just started to learn it...)
- Di dove sei? (Where are you from?) (Informal)
- Di dove siete? (Where are you from?) (Plural)
- Da dove viene? (Where are you from?) (Formal)
- Sono qui in vacanza. (I'm here on a holiday.)
- Mi piace molto qui. (I like it here very much.)
- Quanti anni hai? (How old are you?) (Informal)
- Note: it is not polite to ask the age of a woman or someone older than you.
- Ho ... anni. (I'm ... years old.)

Numbers

Numbers are a good thing to know, and it's not that hard. If you learn the numbers from 0 to 29 the rest is just the same, quite simple.

Why would you want to know the numbers in Italian you might wonder? Well imagine you're in Italy and want to ask what time the bus comes, you know how to ask it in Italian but people are going to answer in the same language so you need to know how the numbers sound.

So what do you say? Ready to learn?

From 0 to 29

- 0 – zero
- 1 – uno/una
- 2 – due
- 3 – tre
- 4 – quattro
- 5 – cinque
- 6 – sei
- 7 – sette
- 8 – otto
- 9 – nove
- 10 – dieci
- 11 – undici
- 12 – dodici
- 13 – tredici

- 14 – quattordici
- 15 – quindici
- 16 – sedici
- 17 – diciassette
- 18 – diciotto
- 19 – diciannove
- 20 – venti
- 21 – ventuno
- 22 – ventidue
- 23 – ventitré
- 24 – ventiquattro
- 25 – venticinque
- 26 – ventisei
- 27 – ventisette
- 28 – ventotto
- 29 – ventinove

Numbers from 10 to 100 in tens

- 10 – dieci
- 20 – venti
- 30 – trenta
- 40 – quaranta
- 50 – cinquanta
- 60 – sessanta
- 70 – settanta
- 80 – ottanta
- 90 – novanta
- 100 – cento

Large numbers

- 123 - centoventitré
- 200 - duecento
- 300 - trecento
- 400 - quattrocento
- 500 - cinquecento
- 600 - seicento
- 700 - settecento
- 800 - ottocento
- 900 - novecento
- 999 - novecentonovantanove
- 1000 – mille

Directions & Places

Getting lost is never a good thing, but getting lost in a country you don't understand the language is worse, so you need some way to ask for directions.

Let's now learn how to ask for directions in Italian.

- Excuse me, could you tell me how to get to …?(Mi scusi, potrebbe dirmi come arrivare a …?)
- Excuse me, do you know where the … is? (Mi scusi, sa dove si trova …?)
- I'm looking for … (Sto cercando …)
- Are we on the right road for …? (Siamo sulla strada giusta per …?)
- Is this the right way for …? (É la strada giusta per …?)
- Do you have a map?(Avrebbe una mappa?)
- Can you show me on the map? (Può mostrarmelo sulla mappa?)
- Is there a restaurant near here? (C'è un ristorante qua vicino?)
- Where is the nearest drugstore, please? (Mi scusi, dove si trova la farmacia più vicina?)

- Can you tell me how to get to the train station, please? (Mi scusi, può dirmi come arrivare alla stazione?)
- How long will it take to get there? (Quanto tempo ci vuole?)
- Does this bus go downtown? (Questo autobus va in centro?)

It's not enough to ask where something is or how to go to some place, you need to understand the answer, let's see some traffic vocabulary:

- **Left** – sinistra
- **Right** – destra
- **Go along …** – Vai/vada lungo …
- **Cross** – attraversa/attraversi
- **Straight on** – diritto
- **Opposite** – contrario
- **Near** – vicino
- **Next to** – accanto a
- **Between** – tra/fra/in mezzo a
- **At the end (of)** – alla fine (di)
- **On/at the corner** – all'angolo
- **Behind** – dietro
- **In front of** – di fronte a
- **Around the corner** – oltre l'angolo

- **Traffic lights** – semaforo
- **Crossroads** – incrocio

And finally names of places that you might want to find:

- **Supermarket** – supermercato
- **Hospital** – ospedale
- **Store** – negozio
- **City hall** – municipio
- **Bank** – banca
- **Church** – chiesa
- **Square** – piazza
- **Bus stop** – fermata dell'autobus
- **Club** – club (pronounced either as in English or like "cloob")
- **Drugstore** – farmacia
- **Gas station** – distributore/benzinaio
- **Police station** – Polizia
- **School** – scuola
- **College** – università
- **Bakery** – panetteria
- **Snack bar** –bar
- **Library** – biblioteca
- **Museum** – museo

Transportation

When you go to a foreign country you most likely are going to take public transport at some point, so you need to know the vocabulary.

Let's learn the different types of transport and some transport vocabulary.

Travelling Vocabulary

- Where's the ticket office? – Dov'è la biglietteria?
- Where do I get the ... to Southampton? – Dove prendo il/l' ... per Southampton?
- What time's the next ... to Portsmouth? – A che ora passa il prossimo ...per Portsmouth?
- This ... has been cancelled – Questo... è stato cancellato
- This ... has been delayed – Questo... è in ritardo
- Have you ever been to ...? – Sei mai stato a...?
- Yes, I went there on holiday – Sì, ci sono stato in vacanza
- No, I've never been there – No, non ci sono mai stato

- I've never been, but I'd love to go someday – Non ci sono mai stato, ma mi piacerebbe andarci un giorno
- How long does the journey take? – Quanto dura il viaggio?
- What time do we arrive? – A che ora arriviamo?
- Do you get travel sick? – Soffri il mal d'auto? (by car)
- Do you get travel sick? – Soffri il mal d'aria? (by plane)
- Do you get travel sick? – Soffri il mal di mare? (by boat)
- Have a good journey! – Fa' buon viaggio!
- Enjoy your trip! – Divertiti!
- I'd like to travel to … - Mi piacerebbe andare in…
- I'd like to book a trip to … - Vorrei prenotare un viaggio per/in…
- How much are the flights to …? – Quanto costano i voli per …?
- Do you have any brochures on …? – Avete dei depliant …?

- Do I need a visa for …? – C'è bisogno del visto per …?

Means of Transportation

- (aero)plane(s) – aereo/i
- (bi)cycle(s) – bici(cletta/e)
- Boat(s) – barca/che
- Bus(es) - autobus
- Car(s) – macchina/e
- Helicopter(s) – elicottero/i
- lorry(lorries) – camion
- Moped(s) - scooter
- (motor)bike(s) - moto
- Ship(s) – nave/i
- Submarine(s) / sub(s) – sottomarino/i
- Tanker(s) – petroliera/e
- Taxi(s) - taxi
- Train(s) – treno/i
- Tram(s) – tram
- Tube train(s)/underground train(s) - metro
- Van(s) - camper
- Yacht(s) – yacht

Let's learn some additional phrases:

Taxi

- Do you know where I can get a taxi? – Sa/sai dove posso prendere un taxi?
- Do you have a taxi number? – Ha/hai il numero di un taxi

- Hello, I need a taxi – Salve, avrei bisogno di un taxi
- Sorry, there are none available at the moment – Mi dispiace, al momento non ce n'è nessuno disponibile
- Where are you? – Dove sei?
- What's the address? – Qual è l'indirizzo?
- I'm ... - Sono...
  - at the Metropolitan Hotel – al Metropolitan
  - at the train station – alla stazione (dei treni)
- How long will it be? – Quanto ci vuole?
  - quarter of an hour – un quarto d'ora
  - about ten minutes – circa dieci minuti
- Where do you need to go? – Dove deve andare?
  - I need to go ... - Devo andare...
  - Could you take me to ...? – Può portarmi a...?
- Could we stop at a cashpoint? – Possiamo fermarci a un bancomat?
- Is the meter switched on? – Il tassimetro è in funzione?

- How much would it cost? – Quanto viene/costa?
- Please, switch the meter on – Per favore, faccia partire il tassimetro
- How long will the journey take? – Quanto dura il viaggio?
- Do you mind if I open/close the window? – Le dispiace se apro/chiudo il finestrino?
- Are we almost there? – Ci siamo quasi?
- That's fine, keep the change – Non importa, tenga il resto
- Would you like a receipt? – Vuole la ricevuta?
- Note: always ask for the receipt of any transaction.
- Could you pick me up here at ...? – Può venire a prendermi a...?
- Could you wait for me here? – Può aspettarmi qui?

Bus and Train

At the bus or train station

- Where's the ticket office? – Dov'è la biglietteria?

- Where are the ticket machines? – Dove sono le biglietterie/macchinette automatiche?
- What time's the next bus/train to …? – A che ora parte il prossimo autobus/treno per… ?
- Can I buy a ticket on the bus/train? – Posso fare il biglietto sull'autobus/treno?
- Note: as a general rule, buying a ticket on the bus/train will be slightly more expensive.
- How much is a ticket to London? – Quanto costa un biglietto per Londra?
- I'd like a ticket to Bristol – Vorrei un biglietto per Bristol
- When would you like to travel? – Dove vuole andare?

When will you be coming back? – Quando intende tornare?

- I'd like a return to …, coming back on Sunday – Vorrei un biglietto di andata e ritorno per …, con ritorno di domenica.
- Where is the platform for…? – Dov'è il binario per …?
- Is this the right platform for …? –È questo il binario per…?
- Where do I change for …? – Dove devo cambiare per…?

- You'll need to change at ... - Deve cambiare a...
- Can I have a timetable, please? – Posso avere un orario, per favore?
- How often do the buses/trains run to ...? – Ogni quanto passano gli autobus/treni per ...?
- The train's running late – Il treno è in ritardo
- The train's been cancelled – Il treno è stato cancellato

On the bus or train

- Does this bus/train stop at ...? – Questo autobus/treno ferma a...?
- Could you tell me when we get to ...? – Può avvisarmi quando stiamo arrivando a...?
- Could you please stop at ...? – Potrebbe fermarsi a...?
- Is this seat free? – È libero?
- Is this seat taken? – È occupato?
- Do you mind if I sit here? – Le dispiace se mi siedo qui?
- Tickets, please – Biglietti, grazie.
- Could I see your ticket, please? – Posso vedere il suo biglietto, per favore?
- I've lost my ticket – Ho perso il biglietto

- What time do we arrive in …? – A che ora arriviamo a…?
- What's this stop? – Che fermata è questa?
- What's the next stop? – Qual è la prossima fermata?
- This is my stop – Questa è la mia fermata
- I'm getting off here – Io scendo qui
- Is there a buffet car on the train? – C'è un vagone ristorante sul treno?
- This train terminates here – Il treno si ferma qui
- Please take all your luggage and personal belongings with you – per favore, prendete tutti i vostri bagagli ed effetti personali.

The Tube/subway

- Could you tell me where the nearest Tube station is? – Può dirmi dove si trova la fermata della metro più vicina?
- Where's there a map of the Underground? – Dove trovo una mappa della metro?
- Which line do I need for Camden Town? – Che linea devo prendere per Camden Town?
- How many stops is it to …? – Quante fermate ci sono per …?

- I'd like a Day Travel card, please – Vorrei un biglietto giornaliero, per favore.
- Note: most subway tickets come in the form of single, 15-trips or monthly tickets. Always ask at the ticket office for your options.
- Which zones? – Che zona?
- Platform – Binario
- Waiting room – Sala d'attesa
- Lost property – Oggetti smarriti
- Underground - Metropolitana
- Bus stop – Fermata dell'autobus
- Request stop – Prenotare la fermata
- On time – In orario
- Delayed – In ritardo
- Cancelled – Cancellato
- Priority seat – Posti riservati

Planes

Checking in

- I've come to collect my tickets – Devo ritirare I biglietti
- I booked on the internet – Ho prenotato su internet
- Do you have your booking reference? – Ha un numero di riferimento?

- Your passport and ticket, please – Passaporto e biglietto, per favore
- Here's my booking reference – Questo è il mio numero di riferimento
- Where are you flying to? – Dove sta andando?
- Did you pack your bags yourself? – Ha impacchettato lei il suo bagaglio?
- Has anyone had access to your bags in the meantime? – Qualcuno ha avuto accesso ai suoi bagagli nel frattempo?
- Do you have any liquids or sharp objects in your hand baggage? – Ci sono liquidi od oggetti appuntiti nel bagaglio a mano?
- How many bags are you checking in? – Quante valigie deve imbarcare?
- Could I see your hand baggage, please? – Potrei vedere il suo bagaglio a mano, per favore?
- Do I need to check this in or can I take it with me? – Devo passarlo al check-in o posso portarlo con me?
- You'll need to check that in – Deve passarlo al check-in
- There's an excess baggage charge of … - Ha un bagaglio in eccesso, c'è un costo addizionale di …

- Would you like a window or an aisle seat? – Preferisce un posto finestrino o sul corridoio?
- Enjoy your flight! - Buon volo!
- Where can I get a trolley? – Dove posso trovare un carrello?

Security
- Are you carrying any liquids? – Ha qualche liquid con sè?
- Could you take off your ..., please? – Potrebbe togliersi il/la ..., per favore?
- Put any metallic objects into the tray, please – Metta tutti gli oggetti metallici nel vassoio, per favore
- Please empty your pockets – Per favore, svuoti le tasche
- Please take your laptop out of its case – Tolga il portatile dalla custodia, per favore
- I'm afraid you can't take that through – Mi dispiace, non può portarlo con sè

In the departure lounge
- What's the flight number? – Qual è il numero del volo?
- Which is our gate? – Qual è il nostro gate?

- Last call for passenger Smith travelling to Miami, please proceed immediately to Gate number 32 – Ultima chiamata per il signor Smith del volo per Miami, dirigersi immediatamente al gate 32, grazie
- The flight's been delayed – Il volo è in ritardo
- The flight's been cancelled – Il volo è stato cancellato
- We'd like to apologise for the delay – Ci scusiamo per il ritardo
- Could I see your passport and boarding card, please? – Potrei vedere il suo passaporto e la sua carta d'imbarco, per favore?

On the plane
- What's your seat number? – Che numero ha?
- Could you please put that in the overhead locker? – Potrebbe metterlo nell'armadietto, per favore?
- Please pay attention to this short safety demonstration – Per favore, prestate attenzione a questa breve dimostrazione delle procedure di sicurezza
- Please turn off all mobile phones and electronic devices – Per favore, spegnete tutti i cellulari e i dispositivi elettronici

- The captain has turned off the Fasten Seatbelt sign – Il capitano ha spento il segnale di allacciare le cinture
- How long does the flight take? – Quanto dura il volo?
- Would you like any food or refreshments? – Gradisce uno snack o una bibita?
- The captain has switched on the Fasten Seatbelt sign – Il capitano ha accesso il segnale di allacciare le cinture
- We'll be landing in about fifteen minutes – Atterreremo in quindici minuti
- Please fasten your seatbelt and return your seat to the upright position – Per favore, allacciate le cinture e portate il sedile in posizione verticale
- Please stay in your seat until the aircraft has come to a complete standstill and the Fasten Seatbelt sign has been switched off – Per favore, rimanete seduti finché l'aereo non è completamente fermo e il segnale di allacciare le cinture non è stato spento
- The local time is ... - L'ora locale è...

Things you might see
- Arrivals - Arrivi

- Departures - Partenze
- International check-in – Check-in internazionale
- Domestic flights – Voli nazionali
- Check-in closes 40 minutes before departure – Il check-in chiude quaranta minuti prima dell'orario di partenza
- Transfers – Trasferimenti
- Baggage claim – Ritiro bagagli
- Passport control – Controllo passaporti
- Customs - Dogana
- Car hire – Affitto macchine

- Gate closed – Gate chiuso

Eating out

Dining Etiquette

If invited to a dinner party in Italy, take into account the following:

- Arrive no more than 15 minutes after the stipulated time.
- You may arrive 15 and 30 minutes later than the stipulated time when invited to a party or other large social gathering.
- Do not discuss business in social situations.
- Always bring a gift to your hosts. A bottle of wine or a dessert are usually fine.
- If you want to bring flowers, do not give chrysanthemums as they are used at funerals.
- Depending on the occasion, table manners may be more or less formal.
- Remain standing until invited to sit down. You may be shown to a particular seat.
- Table manners are continental: the fork is held in the left hand and the knife in the right while eating.

- Do not begin eating until the hostess says "buon appetito".
- Do not rest your elbows on the table, although your hands should be visible at all times.
- Most food is eaten with utensils. Fruit and cheese may be cut with a knife and eaten with your hands.
- Keep your napkin to the left of your plate while eating.
- If you have not finished eating, cross your knife and fork on your plate with the fork over the knife.
- Indicate you have finished eating by laying your knife and fork parallel on your plate, tines facing up, with the handles facing to the left.
- It is acceptable to leave a small amount of food in your plate.

Vocabulary

Eating and drinking

Here are a few expressions you may find useful when arranging to go for a drink or meal, and a couple of signs you may see whilst out.

- Do you know any good restaurants? —Conosci/e qualche buon ristorante?

- Where's the nearest restaurant? – Dove si trova il ristorante più vicino?
- Can you recommend a good pub near here? – Puoi/può consigliarmi un buon pub/bar qui vicino?
- Do you fancy a pint? – Ti/le va una birra?
- Shall we go for a drink? – Ti/le va di bere qualcosa?
- Do you know any good places to …? – Conosci/conosce un buon posto per…?
- Eat – Mangiare
    - get a sandwich – mangiare un panino
    - go for a drink – bere qualcosa

- Shall we get a take-away? – Ordiniamo da asporto/a domicilio?
- Let's eat out tonight – Andiamo a mangiare fuori
- Would you like to …? – Ti/le andrebbe…?
    - come for a drink after work – passa/passi a bere qualcosa dopo il lavoro
    - come for a coffee – passa/passi a prendere un caffè
    - join me for lunch – vieni/venga a pranzo con me

At pub/bar

Ordering drinks

- What would you like to drink? – Cosa ti/le piacerebbe bere?

- What are you having? – Cosa prendi/prende?
- What can I get you? – Cosa posso portarti/portarle?
- I'll have ..., please – Prendo..., per favore.
    - A beer – una birra
    - a glass of white/red wine – un bicchiere di bianco/rosso
    - an orange juice – un succo d'arancia
    - a coffee – un caffè
    - a Coke – una Coca
- Lots of ice, please – molto ghiaccio, per favore
- A little, please – poco, per favore
- Are you being served? – È già stato servito?
- I'm being served, thanks – Sono già stato servito, grazie
- Who's next? – A chi tocca?
- Which wine would you like? – Che vino gradisce?
- House wine is fine – Il vino della casa è molto buono
- I'll have the same, please – Prendo lo stesso, grazie
- Nothing for me, thanks – Per me niente, grazie
- Keep the change! – Tenga il resto
- Are you still serving drinks? – Servite ancora da bere?

Ordering snacks and food
- Do you have any snacks? – Avete degli snack?
- Do you have any sandwiches? – Avete dei panini?
- Do you serve food? – Servite da mangiare?
- What time does the kitchen close? – A che ora chiude la cucina?
- Are you still serving food? – Servite ancora da mangiare?
- What flavour would you like? – a che gusto lo/la/le vuole?
    - really salted – molto salato/a/e
    - cheese and onion – formaggio e cipolla
    - salt and vinegar – sale e aceto
- What sort of sandwiches do you have? – Che panini avete?
- Do you have any hot food? – Servite cibi caldi?
- Today's specials are on the board – Il menù del giorno è segnato sulla lavagna/lavagnetta
- What can I get you? – Cosa posso portarle?
- Would you like anything to eat? – Desidera qualcosa da mangiare?
- Could we see a menu, please? – Potremmo vedere il menù, per favore?

- Eat in or take-away? – Mangi/mangia/mangiate qui o porti/porta/portate via?

Internet access

- Do you have internet access here? – C'è accesso internet qui?
- Do you have wireless internet here? – Avete il wi-fi? (Pronounced "wai-fai")
- What's the password for the internet? – Qual è la password?

Smoking

- Do you smoke? – Fumi/fuma?
- No, I don't smoke – No, non fumo
- Do you mind if I smoke? – Ti/le dispiace se fumo?
- Would you like a cigarette? – Vuoi/vuole una sigaretta?

At a restaurant

These phrases will help you to make a reservation at a restaurant and order your meal. On arrival it is customary to wait to be seated. Service charge is included and it is not necessary to leave a tip.

Booking a table

- Do you have any free tables? – Avete dei tavoli liberi?

- A table for two, please – Un tavolo per due, grazie
- I'd like to make a reservation – Vorrei prenotare
- I'd like to book a table, please – Vorrei prenotare un tavolo
- When for? – Per quando?
- For what time? – Per che ora?
- This evening at … - Per questa sera alle …
- For how many people? – Per quante persone?
- I've got a reservation – Ho una prenotazione
- Do you have a reservation? – Ha una prenotazione/ ha prenotato?

Ordering the meal

- Could I see the menu, please? – Potrei avere un menù, per favore?
- Could I see the wine list, please? – Potrei avere la lista dei vini, per favore?
- Can I get you any drinks? – Posso portarvi qualcosa da bere?
- Are you ready to order? – Siete pronti per ordinare?
- Do you have any specials? – Avete piatti speciali?

- What's the soup of the day? – Qual è la zuppa del giorno?
- What's this dish? – Che piatto è questo?
- What do you recommend? – Cosa mi/ci consiglia?
- I'm a vegetarian – Sono vegetariano/a
- I don't eat ... - Non mangio...
    - Meat – Carne
    - Pork - Porco
- I'll have the ... - Prendo il/la/l'...
    - Chicken breast – petto di pollo
    - Roast beef – arrosto
    - Pasta – pasta
- I'm sorry, we're out of that- Mi dispiace, è terminato.
- For my starter I'll have the soup, and for my main course the steak – Come primo la zuppa e come secondo la bistecca
- How would you like your steak? – Come vuole la bistecca?
    - Rare – al sangue
    - Medium – media
    - well done – ben cotta
- Is that all? – È tutto?
- Would you like anything else? – Desidera ancora qualcosa?

- Nothing else, thank you – Nulla, grazie
- We're in a hurry – Siamo di fretta
- How long will it take? – Quanto ci vorrà all'incirca?

- It'll take about twenty minutes – (Ci vorrà) all'incirca venti minuti

During the meal

If you'd like to get the waiter's attention, make eye contact with them or politely raise your hand. If everything else fails, you can say:

- Excuse me! – Mi scusi!

Here are some other phrases you may hear or wish to use during your meal:

- Enjoy your meal! – Buon appetito!
- Would you like to taste the wine? – Desidera assaggiare il vino?
- Could we have …? – Potremmo avere…?
    - another bottle of wine – un'altra bottiglia di vino
    - some more bread – dell'altro pane
    - some more milk – dell'altro latte
    - a jug of tap water – una caraffa d'acqua
    - some water – dell'acqua

- Would you like any coffee or dessert? – Desidera un dolce o un caffè?
- What desserts do you have? – Che dolci avete?
- Could I see the dessert menu? – Potrei vedere la lista dei dolci?
- Was everything alright? – È stato di vostro gradimento?
- Thanks, that was delicious – Era tutto buonissimo, grazie

Problems
- This isn't what I ordered – Non è quello che ho ordinato
- This food's cold – Il cibo è freddo
- This is too salty – È troppo salato
- This doesn't taste right – Ha un sapore strano
- We've been waiting a long time – È molto che aspettiamo
- Excuse me, is our meal on its way? – Mi scusi, i nostri piatti stanno arrivando?
- Will our food be long? – Ci vorrà ancora molto?

Paying the bill
- The bill, please – Il conto, per favore

- Could we have the bill, please? – Potremmo avere il conto, per favore?
- Can I pay by card? – Posso pagare con carta?
- Do you take credit cards? – Accettate carte di credito?
- Can we pay separately? – Possiamo pagare separatamente?

Hotel and Accommodation

These expressions may come in useful when choosing an accommodation.

- Can you recommend any good ...? – Può consigliarmi un buon...?
    - Hotels - hotel
    - B&Bs – bed and breakfast
    - youth hostels - ostello
    - campsites – campeggio
- How many stars does it have? – Quante stelle ha?
- I'd like to stay in the city centre – Vorrei rimanere nel centro
- How much do you want to pay? – Quanto vuole spendere?
- How far is it from the ...? – Quanto dista dal/dalla...?
    - city centre – centro città
    - airport - aeroporto
    - station – stazione

Making a reservation

These are some of the phrases you will need when making a hotel reservation.

Checking availability

- Do you have any vacancies? – Avete delle camere libere?

- From what date? – Per che data?
- For how many nights? – Per quante notti?
- How long will you be staying for? – Per quanto si ferma?
    - one night – una notte
    - a week – una settimana
    - a fortnight – due settimane
- What sort of room would you like? – Che tipo di camera desidera?
- I'd like a ... - Vorrei...
    - single room – una singola
    - double room – una doppia
- I'd like a room with ... - Vorrei una camera con
    - an en-suite bathroom – bagno
    - a bath – vasca da bagno
    - a shower –doccia
    - a view – vista
    - a balcony - balcone
- Could we have an extra bed? – Potremmo avere un letto in più?

Asking about facilities

- Does the room have ...? – La camera ha...?
    - internet access – accesso a internet
    - air conditioning – aria condizionata

- television - la televisione
- Is there a ...? – Disponete di ...?
    - swimming pool - piscina
    - sauna - sauna
    - gym - palestra
    - beauty salon – salone di bellezza/spa
    - lift - ascensore
- Do you allow pets? – Gli animali sono ammessi?
- Do you have wheelchair access? – Avete accesso per i disabili?
- Do you have a car park? – Avete un parcheggio?
- The room has a shared bathroom – La camera ha il bagno in comune

Discussing terms

- What's the price per night? – Qual è il costo per una notte?
- Is breakfast included? – La colazione è inclusa?
- That's a bit more than I wanted to pay – È più di quanto vorrei spendere
- Can you offer me any discount? – Può farmi uno sconto?
- Have you got anything ...? – Avete qualcosa di più...?

- o Cheaper -economico
- o Bigger – grande
- o Quieter - tranquillo
- Could I see the room? – Potrei vedere la camera?

Making the Booking

- OK, I'll take it – D'accordo, accetto
- I'd like to make a reservation – Vorrei fare una prenotazione
- What's your name, please? – Può dirmi il suo nome?
- Can I take your ...? – Può darmi il suo...?
    - o credit card number – numero di carta di credito
    - o telephone number – numero di telefono

Checking in

On arrival at your hotel these expressions will help you when checking in.

- I've got a reservation – Ho una prenotazione
- Your name, please? – Il suo nome, per favore?
- Could I see your passport? – Posso vedere il suo passaporto?

- Could you please fill in this registration form? – Compili il registro, per favore
- My booking was for a double room – avevo prenotato una camera doppia
- Would you like a newspaper? – Vuole un giornale?
- What time's breakfast? – A che ora servite la colazione?
- Breakfast's from 7am till 10am – La colazione viene servita dalle sette alle dieci
- Could I have breakfast in my room, please? – Potrei avere la colazione in camera, per favore?
- What time's the restaurant open for dinner? – A che ora servite la cena?
- Dinner's served between 6pm and 9.30pm – La cena viene servita dalle sei alle nove e mezza (di sera)
- What time does the bar close? – A che ora chiude il bar?
- Would you like any help with your luggage? – Ha bisogno di aiuto con I bagagli?
- Here's your room key – Questa è la sua chiave
- Your room number's ... - La sua/vostra camera è la numero...
- Your room's on the first floor – La sua/vostra camera è al primo piano

- Where are the lifts? - Dove sono gli ascensori?
- Enjoy your stay! – Buona permanenza!

Things you might see

- Do not disturb – Non disturbare
- Please make up room – Per favore fate spazio
- Lift out of order – Ascensore fuori servizio

Checking out

These English phrases will be useful when checking out of a hotel.

- I'd like to check out – Vorrei fare il check-out
- I'd like to pay my bill, please – Vorrei pagare il conto
- I think there's a mistake in this bill – Credo che ci sia un errore nel conto
- How would you like to pay? – Come preferisce pagare?
- Have you used the minibar? – Ha usato il minibar?
- Could we have some help bringing our luggage down? – Ci servirebbe una mano a portare giù i bagagli
- Do you have anywhere we could leave our luggage? – C'è un posto dove possiamo lasciare i bagagli?

- Could I have a receipt, please? – Posso avere la ricevuta?
- Could you please call me a taxi? – Potrebbe chiamarmi un taxi, per favore?
- I hope you had an enjoyable stay – Spero che si sia trovato bene da noi
- I've really enjoyed my stay – Mi sono trovato molto bene

Shopping

Whether you love shopping, or just shop when you need to, you can practice your Italian at the same time!

Shopping is a great way to communicate with lots of different people, and it really helps to boost your confidence in speaking Italian!

If you familiarise yourself with the phrases and vocabulary in this book, then you'll know what you should expect to hear from the people you talk to on your shopping spree. It'll make shopping a more enjoyable experience, and improve your Italian too!

Opening times

- What times are you open? – A che ora aprite?
- We're open from 9am to 5pm, Monday to Friday – Siamo aperti dalle nove di mattina alle cinque del pomeriggio, da lunedì a venerdì.
- We're open from 10am to 8pm, seven days a week – Siamo aperti dalle dieci di mattina alle otto di sera, sette giorni su sette
- Are you open on …? – Siete aperti di…?
- What time do you close? – A che ora chiudete?

- What time do you close today? – A che ora chiudete oggi?
- What time do you open tomorrow? – A che ora aprite domani?

Selecting goods

- Can I help you? – Posso aiutarla?
- I'm just browsing, thanks – Sto solo dando un'occhiata, grazie.
- How much is this? – Quanto viene/costa?
- How much are these? – Quanto vengono/costano?
- How much is that … in the window? – Quanto viene/costa quel/quella … in vetrina?
- That's cheap – Non costa molto.
- That's good value – È un buon prezzo.
- That's expensive – È caro.
- Do you sell …? – Vendete …?
- Sorry, we don't sell them – Mi dispiace, non li vendiamo.
- Sorry, we don't have any left – Mi dispiace, li abbiamo esauriti.
- I'm looking for … - Sto cercando…
- Could you tell me where the … is? – Può dirmi dov'è/dove sono?

- Where can I find the …? – Dove posso trovare…?
- Have you got anything cheaper? – Avete qualcosa di più economico?
- It's not what I'm looking for – Non è ciò che sto cercando.
- Do you have this item in stock? – Disponete di …?
- Does it come with a guarantee? – Ha la garanzia?
- Do you deliver? – Consegnate a domicilio?
- I'll take this - Prendo questo.
- Would you like anything else? – Desidera altro?
- Will that be all? – Basta così?

Making payment
- Are you in the queue? – È/siete in fila?
- Next, please! – A chi tocca?
- Do you take credit cards? – Accettate carte di credito?
- I'll pay in cash – Pago in contanti
- I'll pay by card – Pago con carta
- Could I have a receipt, please? – Posso avere la ricevuta, per favore?

- Would you be able to gift wrap it for me? – Può farmi una confezione regalo?
- Would you like a bag? – Vuole una busta/borsa?

Returns and complaints

- I'd like to return this – Vorrei restituire questo
- I'd like to change this for a different size – Vorrei cambiarlo con una taglia diversa
- It doesn't work – Non funziona
- It doesn't fit – Non mi entra/sta
- Could I have a refund? – Posso avere un rimborso?
- Have you got the receipt? – Ha la ricevuta?
- Could I speak to the manager? – Potrei parlare con il direttore/con un superiore?

Things you might see

- Open - Aperto
- Closed - Chiuso
- Open 24 hours a day – Aperto 24 ore su 24
- Special offer – Offerta speciale
- Sale - Sconto
- Buy 1 get 1 free – Comprane uno, ne ricevi uno in omaggio
- Half price – Metà prezzo

- Out to lunch – Pausa pranzo
- Back in 15 minutes – Di ritorno in 15 minuti
- Shoplifters will be prosecuted – Il furto è perseguibile a norma di legge

Using a credit card
- Enter your PIN – Inserisca il PIN
- Please wait – Attenda, per favore/prego
- Remove card – Ritiri la carta
- Signature – Firma

**** PREVIEW OTHER BOOKS BY THIS AUTHOR****

"Rome Travel Guide for Women" by Erica Stewart

Excerpt from the first Chapter

Chapter 1: What to Know Before You Go

The urge to be spontaneous, book a cheap flight to Rome and go with the flow may seem romantic and enticing at first thought. Yet ask anyone who's actually tried that and they're likely to bring you back down to earth. Romantic spontaneity is one thing, yet visiting this sprawling metropolis of 2.5 million inhabitants and over 4 million tourists a year, with nothing more than a wing and a prayer – even if that prayer is uttered in the Vatican City - will likely leave you exhausted, frustrated and with not much time on your hands. We're not saying a trip to Rome needs to be approached with German-style military precision, yet it pays to know a little of what to expect, what to avoid and what to keep in mind.

So here's our ultimate list of all we think you should know...before you go.

You can't do it, see it and eat it all

Try as you may, you'll NEVER be able to 'do' Rome in a single visit, so the sooner you accept this fact the better your planning will go. Everything about a visit here is about prioritizing, whether it be attractions, restaurants, dishes or shopping strips. As the saying goes 'Rome was not built in a day' and only the delusional could ever believe they could see it all over a long weekend. Moreover, do you know why so many people are hopelessly in love with the Eternal City? Because they know they can visit once a year, for two decades, and *still* find plenty to see and do. There's a very good reason for that. Rome will offer you 1001 reasons to come back, time and time again. Let her work her magic on you as well.

Which brings us to our next point...

When in Rome, do as the Romans do. Prioritize!

A vacation in Rome may well be a once-in-a-lifetime luxury for many yet even if there is no chance in sight of visiting a second time, you'll still need to prioritize your most fervent wishes in order of preference. Is there a church, an ancient site or a restaurant you've been dying to visit for years? Then put THAT at the top of your list and head forth every day with your list in your pocket. Yes, we know, it's not awfully adventurous to tick items off lists, but if you don't want to head home with more regrets than unforgettable moments, you'd do well to compile a list of your must-dos. Crossing the Mongolian steppe for two weeks on camelback is an adventure; spending your days in Rome walking around like a headless hen because you can't decide what to do first, is just a woeful waste of a golden opportunity. This city is immense, spread out and home to more monuments, museums and landmarks than most other countries. Do yourself a favour: prioritize.

Rome is not nearly as dangerous as it's made out to be. But...

As far as large capital cities are concerned, Rome is no more dangerous than London, New York or Paris, yet also suffers from its fair bout of pickpockets, traps and scams of which you should be aware. By and large, you should be at your most vigilant when in heavily touristy areas and anywhere around the Termini Train Station after sunset. All major transport hubs the world over are quite seedy, but Rome's can be particularly unsavoury, so do have your wits about you. Consolation remains in the fact that overpricing and petty theft is part of life in any major city and at least here it is not only aimed at tourists. Romans get scammed and pick-pocketed just as often as visitors and keep in mind that they spend much less time in the city's touristy areas. Don't pack your most precious jewellery or handbag and don't walk around with your flashy DLR camera around your neck and hundreds of Euros bulging out of your purse and you'll be much less likely to stand out.

You'll be doing a lot of walking. A LOT of walking.

Rome is not Venice. And, in this particular case, it is not Florence either. Rome is an extremely modern, effervescent city which has been spreading its wings far and wide among its priceless ruins for thousands of years. Unfortunately, when Roman Emperors erected their temples, churches, columns and amphitheatres, they had very little regards for what that would mean to tourists a millennia or two later. All of the city's major (and minor) landmarks and highlights are spread out far and wide and across seven vertiginous hills. Considering the rather pesky public transport system (more on this later) to make the best of your visit you're going to have to do a lot of walking, most of which will be uphill. This is one aspect of a Roman visit which many first-timers fail to realize. Pack comfy shoes and leave those sexy heels for a city which is flat and boasts no cobblestone alleyways.

Skip the Metro and get acquainted with the public buses

Many visitors to Rome are understandably petrified of hopping on local buses and we really can't blame them. They are often overcrowded, hardly ever run on time (does anything, in Italy?) and the sheer number of bus numbers and routes to memorize are headache-inducing. Getting familiar with a few bus routes and timetables can be a lot of effort for just a few days' visit BUT if you manage to do just that, your rewards will be tremendous. Due to the number of underground crypts in Rome's most historic core (which is extensive enough as it is), the city's underground Metro steers so far from any point of interest as to make it almost completely useless to tourists. Instead, its buses which ply the routes across the centre. Hopping on them will save you infinite time and leg-ache. One uphill walk saved a day can go a long way in ensuring you don't burn out within just 48 hours of arriving. So channel your inner Roman and learn to love the buses. Pick up a detailed bus timetable from newspaper stands and tobacconists (*tabaccaio* – where you can also purchase bus tickets) and grill your hotel/hostel staff as to all the bus routes to and from your chosen accommodation. Do note that although there are numerous bus passes (for 48 hours or weekly) offered, you are likely never to need them. Single bus tickets cost just €1.50 and are valid for 75 minutes, meaning you can hop on and off different buses at will for 75 minutes after you initially validate your ticket. At most, you will probably only need two tickets a day; considering daily tickets start at €6 they are really not worth the expense. *NB. Bus #64 which plies the tourist route is known locally as the 'pickpocket express' so avoiding it altogether would be a wise move.*

Pre-planning is ideal

In today's technologically savvy times, there's a bunch of research you can do online before you even arrive, saving you loads of precious vacation time. Download a detailed map of Rome, make sure to note not just distances but walking times (you won't find many maps which denote hills etc) and get acquainted with the bus travel calculator on Google Maps. Surprisingly, this is a lot more efficient than trying to navigate your way through the official ATAC online website. Remember to never rely on travel times as Rome's at-times congested traffic is the only thing which will determine that.

Steer clear of taxis

Rated among the most unscrupulous in all of Europe,

taxi drivers in Rome have the uncanny skill of taking the 'Every road leads to Rome' credo to frustratingly new highs. The longest possible driving point between A and B? Yes, they will find it and they will charge you through the nose for it. Best bet? Avoid them (almost) at all costs, especially for getting to and from Fiumicino airport.

Pick the right time to visit

The months of June, July and August are tourist high-season in Rome yet note that this is simply a reflection of European summer school holiday times. The very best months to visit the Italian capital, in fact, are either immediately before or immediately after the summer. April and May, together with September and October are simply splendid and ideal months to visit a city which necessitates so much walking and sightseeing. The scorching summer heat has either not yet arrived or already dissipated, and crowds (although still ever present) will be greatly diminished. Other very popular times (which should be avoided by those on tight budgets and with an aversion to crowds) are Christmas time and Easter Week. Only those who are gluttons for punishment should plan to visit the Vatican City – or any other major landmark - on a Sunday.

Be cunning about WHERE you choose to stay

Rome is both compact and spread out depending on your point of view and affinity for long walks. Walking, by the way, is an incredibly enjoyable activity here as every corner and nook of this glorious city hides ancient treasures and priceless relics. It's fair to assume that you don't want to be too far from the action, but this should not mean that your hotel need be right outside the gates of the Colosseum, far from it. The most interesting hoods to stay in are actually *Trastevere*, the latest *rione* to be gentrified and brimming with cool little cafes' and charming boutiques (not to mention THE best Sunday fleamarket in town) and *San Lorenzo*, which is abuzz with young students from the nearby university, and where you'll find the best value-for-money accommodation, dining and drinking options. These areas are particularly ideal for those who want a bit of nightlife right outside their front door. The cheapest area of all is near the Termini Station, but given its insalubrious reputation it is not recommended for ladies travelling alone. The areas around *Piazza Navona* and *Piazza di Spagna* are some of the most popular so tend to be pricier, yet for sheer convenience and elegant ambience they simply can't be beaten.

Load up on fresh, free drinking water

It's all very well to spend weeks on end waiting for that airline ticket to drop by 20 bucks, or begging that hotel manager to include a meagre breakfast with your room rate at no extra charge. But, invariably, you are going to be dropping hundreds and more on expenses you'd probably never envisaged. Drinking water would have to be one of the most overpriced 'luxury' in Rome's tourist centre, due local traders banking on the fact that tourists will avoid the very potable drinking fountains found everywhere in Rome. Don't! The city's *fontanelle* (drinking fountains) have been supplying local inhabitants for thousands of years through ancient Roman aqueducts. Unless you see a sign which says 'non potabile' then go ahead and fill your water bottle with what is, in our humble opinion, the freshest and tastiest drinking water in town.

Need more invaluable insider's info?

Here you go!

Learn (even a little) of the local lingo

It really pays to learn a few Italian phrases before visiting Rome. Italians are not renowned for their command of the English language and, to be brutally honest, many get stroppy if they feel like they should learn a foreign language for the good of tourists.

However, you'll be astonished to discover just how friendly and helpful locals can be, the moment you make even the itziest of efforts to communicate in the local lingo. Start every conversation with a *'Buongiorno, come sta?'* (Hello, how are you?) and don't forget to throw in a few *'per favore'* (please) and *'grazie mille'* (thanks a lot) in there for good measure. Before long, you'll find local Romani to be very accommodating indeed. Along with your linguistic education, may as well add the word *'sciopero'* to your vocabulary. This means 'strike' in Italian, it occurs rather too often and usually involves buses, trains and planes.

Opening/Closing times are – more often than not – purely hypothetical

You've finally sussed out an ideal leather shoes outlet store that you absolutely must visit, even if it means hopping on three different buses and spending four hours of your precious day just getting there. You've checked their site online, know it is open and will just get going, right? Wrong! Before you go to any kind of major effort to visit a place/shop/museum/restaurant do make sure that it is, in fact, open. There are some very valid reasons why Swiss are renowned for their punctuality and the Italians not so much! Although *most* major attractions do try their best to operate within their set times, many independent businesses do not, so unless you want to waste your time and cause yourself unnecessary aggravation, source out a phone number and ask a local (be it your new friend at your local café or hotel concierge) to call ahead and confirm.

Plan on getting lost

Well, it's bound to happen sooner or later and although getting hopelessly lost in Rome can be part of the fun, it can also be part of the stress. Always carry a map of Rome with you and the name and address of your accommodation. When asking for directions, do note that Italians are reputedly bad at giving them (this remains a mystery to so many) so don't rely on just one piece of advice. Gather three and go with the majority.

Fight the urge to rent a scooter or – heaven forbid – a car

No matter how many times you've seen La Dolce Vita, do not – and we repeat do not- be tempted to rent a scooter or a car when in Rome. Driving in and around this city necessitates nerves of steel, knowledge of at least half a dozen obscene Italian hand gestures and a very deep religious belief in Padre Pio. Unless you were born in Italy, in which case all of the above-mentioned traits are embedded into your DNA...Do.Not.Drive.

Ditch the guidebook after two days

Visiting Rome and avoiding the Colosseum, Roman Forum or the Vatican would be an absolute travesty and by all means we would never suggest you do that. However, after you have a few of the main sites covered, do put your book away and let your eyes do the guiding. Some of the most magnificent churches are ones which are never mentioned in guide books, including this one! In Rome, even the most inconspicuous little church can hide a Michelangelo and utterly mesmerizing crypts, so walk into every single church, villa, garden or ruin site you come by and you'll be surprised at the treasures you can find.

Skip the tourist foodie traps

Just because Italy and Rome, in particular, is renowned as a foodie haven it does not mean that every meal in every restaurant is going to leave your taste buds jumping for joy. Quite the opposite is true. By and large, it's worth remembering that no restaurant worth its weight in gnocchi will ever employ waiters to stand outside and try to lure diners in, so if you come across one of these near popular piazzas, you'd do well to keep on walking. Generally speaking, the best food in Rome is served in small, family-run places usually hidden in side alleyways with nay a single white table cloth or waiter uniform in sight. Moreover, every Roman resident thinks he or she knows the very bestest little joint in town, so don't be afraid to ask recommendations from everyone you come across who (obviously) speaks a little English. In a city like Rome, personal recommendations are still the most tried and trusted method of sourcing out the most authentic places. Also worth noting that just because a restaurant is not rated on TripAdvisor, it does not mean it serves bad food. Perhaps, quite the opposite is true. If you come across a lovely looking *trattoria*, full of famished locals beaming happily at a plate of *amatriciana*, then don't be afraid to step right in. But do check prices before you order!

Don't be a tourist!

Yes, you ARE a tourist, but this does not mean you should break the gastronomic cardinal sins of your host country. There's no point going to all sorts of efforts to learn a bit of the lingo and look the part, when you order a *cappuccino* at 3 pm or ask for parmesan cheese for your *marinara*. Mamma mia! Italy is very strict on its food etiquette so know that cappuccino is never ordered past 11 am and never, under any circumstances, should you sprinkle parmesan on any seafood dish. There are a few countries all over the world which boast very strong cuisine cultures, Italy being one of them. Bar what is offered at the table (freshly cracked pepper at most) do not alter a dish with any condiment, lest you risk offending the chef.

Be a Tourist!

No matter what anyone says, head to Rome and skip the Colosseum and you shall be kicking yourself 'till all eternity. The Vatican, Pantheon, Colosseum and Roman Forum are the Holy Trinity(+one!) of Roman sightseeing and an absolute must. An insanely crowded, frustrating must but a must nonetheless. We recommend you visit first thing in the morning and although you can certainly combine the Colosseum and the Forum in one day, the Vatican should really be the highlight on a separate day. Once you have these under your belt, you'll feel free and happy to experience every other treasure this city has to offer.

Skip the line at the Vatican

With most attractions in Rome, it's not worth paying more for a pre-purchased ticket online, yet this is an absolute must for the Vatican City. This is a separate and independent country, so a visit here is not included in any kind of tourist pass in Rome. Pre-purchase your ticket directly from the Vatican Museums Online Ticket Office and skip those heat stroke inducing queues. You will pay about €5 extra, but the privilege of skipping the line is worth every single cent. Don't worry if you arrive later than your predetermined 'visiting time', the Vatican City is not much of a stickler for punctuality either. Your ticket will include entry into the Vatican Museums and the Sistine Chapel, but St Peter's Basilica can only be visited on a tour, so make sure to book that as well. Do note the Vatican has a strict, modest dress code so make sure your shoulders are covered and your skirt/pants end below the knees.

Excerpt from the first Chapter

Printed in Great Britain
by Amazon